Original title:
The Balcony Eden

Copyright © 2025 Creative Arts Management OÜ
All rights reserved.

Author: Gideon Barrett
ISBN HARDBACK: 978-1-80581-760-4
ISBN PAPERBACK: 978-1-80581-287-6
ISBN EBOOK: 978-1-80581-760-4

Petal Paradise

In a garden where daisies dance,
Gnomes take their chance to prance.
Bees wear sunglasses, buzzing loud,
As flowers gossip, feeling proud.

A rogue squirrel tries to steal a shoe,
While butterflies paint the sky so blue.
In this chaos, laughter blooms,
And nature hums its silly tunes.

The Colorful Crossroads

At a corner where colors clash,
Sunflowers cheer as chickens dash.
Jellybeans rain from above,
As kittens meow, spread the love.

A jester frog plays violin,
While ants in hats do a little spin.
This crossroads is quite absurd,
Where nonsense reigns, it's never blurred.

Time Stops at the Edge

At the brink where time takes a break,
Pigs fly high, for goodness' sake!
A clock tower sings a silly tune,
As stars giggle, lighting the moon.

Here, moments stretch like taffy sweet,
While turtles race with nimble feet.
Time forgot how to be serious,
In this place that's just delirious.

A Clutch of Flora

A bunch of plants have formed a band,
With pots and pans, they take a stand.
Fern strums lute, and cactus claps,
While violets offer silly raps.

Snapdragons joke, and lilies laugh,
While weeds try hard to join the staff.
This flora calls, come join the fun,
In their leafy world, we all are one.

Whimsy Above the Pavement

A cat in a hat sings a tune,
While squirrels do choreography under the moon.
The pigeons join in, a tap-dancing crew,
As passersby laugh, unsure what to do.

A dog on a skateboard zooms through the scene,
Chasing down dreams, just like in a dream.
A slice of pizza floats past on a kite,
With toppings of laughter, oh what a sight!

An Invitation to Wonder

A teapot spills secrets, one cup at a time,
While daisies debate if they're post or prime.
Goldfish in top hats take a stroll on the breeze,
Wearing sunglasses, they sip tea with such ease.

The sun winks at clouds in a feathered ballet,
As rainbows jump rope in a colorful fray.
So come join the party, don't be shy or coy,
Where even the shadows dance with pure joy!

Fantasies on the Outcrop

An octopus juggles while riding a bike,
With starfish applauding, what a fun hike!
A moonbeam whispers jokes to the trees,
While flowers giggle, swaying in the breeze.

The clouds wear pajamas, they're taking a nap,
While rabbits in bow ties plan a cool trap.
It's laughter that echoes through valleys and hills,
In a world of delight, with whimsical thrills!

Daydreaming in the Open Air

A monkey in slippers plays chess with the sky,
As cucumbers read novels while learning to fly.
The sun sprinkles laughter like confetti so bright,
While clouds toss and tumble, just enjoying the flight.

Pandas in capes host a dance on the breeze,
With owls doing ballet, they aim to please.
So grab a good joke and come join the cheer,
For the world's a big circus when whimsy draws near!

Solace in Nature's Corners

In a nook where wildflowers bloom,
Sunlight giggles in each room.
Bees are buzzing, not a care,
While ladybugs twirl in the air.

Squirrels prance with acorn flair,
Wishing they could braid their hair.
Birds hold concerts 'neath the trees,
Raccoons chuckle with the breeze.

A Tapestry of Leaves

Leaves are tossing in delight,
Doing flips left and right.
Each branch a stage, each twig a bar,
Nature's fun, a wild bazaar.

Trees wear coats of vibrant hues,
Dancing socks, they can't refuse.
Chirping birds and rustling grass,
Nature's humor, none can surpass.

Hopes Lifted Higher

Kites soar up, much like our dreams,
Tangled in laughter, bursting at the seams.
Clouds play hide and seek all day,
Their soft fluffiness leads us astray.

Joy leaps forth just like a hare,
Who knew being silly was a dare?
Sunlight splashes, shadows prance,
Each moment a carefree dance.

The Frames of Earth and Sky

Framed in hues of sunset gold,
Whispers of mischief, tales retold.
The horizon giggles, stretches wide,
With frolicking clouds as its guide.

Breezes tease as flowers sway,
Nature's gags keep gloom at bay.
With each end of the fading light,
Stars winking in the cozy night.

Perches of Delight

Up high where the pigeons coo,
I sip my tea, watching the view.
A squirrel steals my crumbs with glee,
He's got more finesse than me.

The plants are gossiping, you see,
They whisper tales of grand jubilee.
A flower tried to flirt with a bee,
But he just buzzed away, quite free.

My neighbor's cat strikes a pose,
Thinks he's in a magazine, I suppose.
With each stretch, he purveys his might,
Unbothered by birds in awkward flight.

Here I laugh with my sunny dreams,
In this perch, life isn't as it seems.
With chocolate snacks that I revere,
I live like a king but shed a tear.

Where Hearts Commune

In the space where laughter flows,
A pair of socks in mismatched rows.
My friends drop by for a quick chat,
While I try to explain a dance with a cat.

We share old tales and new ones spun,
Each awkward laugh brightens the sun.
A toast to moments in mid-air,
As snacks go flying without a care.

The pigeon brigade starts a fight,
Over breadcrumbs in the fading light.
Who knew feathery foes could be so proud?
They strut like peacocks, heads unbowed.

With smiles shared and drinks that spill,
Time tick-tocks, but we feel the thrill.
In this little nook, pure joy finds room,
Where even the plants manage to bloom.

A Threshold of Nature

Here at my door, the world unfolds,
With an array of stories told.
A parrot yells 'hello' to hear,
As I trip on a chatty deer.

The flowers bloom in colors bright,
As bees engage in pollen fights.
A kid rides past on a wild bike,
Shouting, 'Nature isn't what you like!'

A breeze tickles my cheek with flair,
I'm constructing dreams from thin air.
Every leaf flutters like a clue,
To a riddle tangled in morning dew.

So here I stand, with arms wide spread,
At this threshold, all worries shed.
With every giggle, and whimsy rare,
Nature's comedy fills the air.

Glimpses of Abundance

I glance down at my veggie patch,
Where lettuce lingers, but it won't hatch.
Tomatoes blush, refusing to grow,
While the weeds are throwing a show.

The sun chases clouds on parade,
As I argue with a ladybug, unafraid.
"Where's my squash?" I dramatically plead,
It rolls away; it knows I don't need.

The ants march by in a straight line,
They mingle, toil, and sip on brine.
"Do the tomatoes have any proof?"
I ponder aloud, feeling aloof.

With each harvest, I chuckle and sigh,
As my kitchen sits empty, but oh, my!
Who knew chaos could taste so grand,
In this little corner of my land?

The Secret Garden Aflame

In a corner of light, with a twist in the plot,
Marigolds giggle, and daisies have thoughts.
Sneaky squirrels dance, while the roses complain,
"Why don't you try to wear less perfume, Jane?"

Laughter erupts from the bees on their spree,
Chasing sweet nectar, as wild as can be.
A garden's alive, with its own little scheme,
Each petal a joke in this floral-themed dream.

Honeyed Moments on High

Nestled up high, where the clouds like to play,
A gnome spills his tea while the sun rays betray.
The wind tells a story, as laughter takes flight,
Tickling the leaves till they giggle with fright.

Birds chirp to serenade, cozy up, take a guess,
In this quirky café, you'd never want less.
With honeyed delights and a sweet little song,
Every silly moment just feels oh-so-wrong.

Breathing in the Views

Sipping on lemonade, with shades on my face,
I'm scaling the heights, in this cozy, calm space.
The daisies salute me, with petals all bright,
While the clouds propose pranks in the soft morning light.

A butterfly flutters, then steals my last fry,
As I shout, "Hey, buddy! You think you can fly?"
With laughter afoot, and a chirp in the air,
I breathe in the views, full of whimsy and flair.

An Oasis of Solitude

In my secret retreat, where the sun's rays collide,
I hold court with the cacti, and I'm filled with pride.
"Bring your best cactus jokes!" I call to the breeze,
As tumbleweeds chuckle, such a light-hearted tease.

Lizards lounge lazily, cracking up at my puns,
While I sip on my beverage, counting the suns.
This oasis of laughter, where solitude thrives,
Leaves me smiling and blissful, in this world that jives.

Hidden Gems in the Air

Up high where birds take flight,
I found a sock, what a sight!
It danced like it was on a dare,
A hidden gem out in the air.

Clouds chuckle, they're all in glee,
As ants march on, what a spree!
A picnic spread with crumbs galore,
While squirrels peek, always wanting more.

The wind whispers, 'What's the catch?'
My lemonade, watch it snatch!
Lemonade that's way too sweet,
A pesky bee claims victory neat.

Up here, the sun plays games so sly,
Tickling toes, oh my, oh my!
With a twist and a twirl, I'll sway,
Hidden gems in a laugh today.

A Canvas of Sky and Blossom

The sky's a canvas, oh what fun,
With doodles drawn by everyone.
A flower's hat, a leaf's ballet,
   Colorful chaos in a cliche.

Butterflies critique the view,
While daisies gossip, oh so blue.
Painting dreams on breezy trails,
As petals hitchhike on the gales.

A cloud shaped like a lazy cat,
Says, 'Hey there, where you at?'
As bees join in to do a jig,
In this garden, so big, so big!

But in this art, a chaos reigns,
With pollen stuck on where it rains.
Each bloom's a laugh, each hue a joke,
On a canvas grand, laughter's spoke.

Heartbeats in Bloom

Petals pulse like beats at night,
Each bloom's a giggle, pure delight.
With chattering leaves in the breeze,
Heartbeats dance between the trees.

The tulips waltz in pairs of two,
While daisies form a funny crew.
With sunshine's glow, they wiggle wide,
Heartbeats thump, our joy can't hide.

Bumblebees buzz like tiny cars,
Racing 'round beneath the stars.
If flowers could laugh, they'd roar and cheer,
Each heartbeat sounds like giggles near.

A parade of colors, wild and loud,
In nature's heart, we're all so proud.
With every sway, a tale of fun,
Heartbeats in bloom, our song's begun!

Swaying with the Wind

In this place, where all things spin,
I tip my hat, let the laughs begin.
The trees all dance, a wobbly show,
Swaying with the wind, to and fro.

A dandelion's spinning tale,
Floats past my nose, oh what a fail!
As giggles ride on each soft breeze,
With every gust, we're tickled with ease.

The hammock sways, it knows the game,
It's not just me, I'm not to blame!
While grasshoppers hop, with little flair,
Each leap, a chuckle, fills the air.

So here we sway, in pure delight,
In nature's joke, it feels so right.
With laughter loud, and breezes bold,
Swaying with the wind, our fun unfolds.

Crescendo of Fluttering Wings

A pigeon perched with lofty dreams,
Nods its head with clumsy schemes.
It coos a tune, an offbeat song,
While dancing where it doesn't belong.

A butterfly floats in a silly chase,
Tickling flowers with its grace.
It trips on petals, spins around,
As grinning bees look on, spellbound.

A squirrel leaps with acrobatic flair,
Chasing shadows without a care.
It slips on leaves, tumbles down,
Landing safely without a frown.

In this garden's silliness unleashed,
Nature's laughter never ceased.
With every flap and leap they bring,
A joyful, funny, feathered fling.

Awakening the Hidden Flora

A cactus wearing a tiny hat,
Sips water through a silk cravat.
It sways with charm in sunlight's glow,
While giggling petals steal the show.

A daisy dons a dapper tie,
Challenging the wind to a butterfly.
It pretends to be an elegant chap,
Then folds up tight for a little nap.

A tulip twirls in a dizzy dance,
Inviting bees for a silly prance.
But they buzz past without a glance,
Leaving her alone in a floral trance.

Underneath this jesting sun,
Flora laughs, it's all in fun.
With every bloom, a smile appears,
Awakening joy amid our cheers.

Whispers of a Sunlit Terrace

On the terrace where the sunlight plays,
A cat sprawls out in lazy displays.
It dreams of fish, on clouds it floats,
While sunbeams tickle its little toes.

A flower pot chatters with gossip galore,
About the squirrel who stole a score.
"I saw him with acorns by the tree,"
Said the basil to the laughing cherry.

A chair creaks with a joke to share,
As the wind whispers secrets in the air.
It leans to a table, "Can you believe?"
They chuckle together, never naive.

In this sunlit place where laughter flows,
Every moment a giggle grows.
With nature's fun at its very best,
On this terrace, we find our rest.

Serenity Above the Cityscape

High above where pigeons mingle,
A rooftop garden starts to jingle.
A parrot with a top hat sings,
Creating laughs with flapping wings.

The sun peeks over the urban tide,
While plants sway like they're on a ride.
A tomato shimmies, rumbles low,
As if to join the city show.

A gnome on watch, so stout and proud,
Yells at clouds that form a crowd.
"You can't rain on my parade today!"
He gestures, causing them to sway.

Amidst the city, comedy reigns,
Even in the most mundane strains.
From rooftops high, life's quirks appear,
In this serene spot, laughter's near.

A Refuge in the Sky

I sit upon my ledge quite high,
With snacks and soda, oh me, oh my!
The squirrels salute with acorn hats,
My royal subjects—how about that?

A bird lands next, quite bold and spry,
He squawks about his daring fly.
I offer crumbs, he takes a nibble,
As I watch, I can't help but giggle.

The sun peeks in, a playful tease,
It warms my toes as I sip with ease.
From up here, the world seems so small,
Just me, my snacks, and a squirrel brawl!

In my sky lounge, laughter rings,
Who knew these heights could hold such things?
With each funny tale from my furry friend,
I find myself wishing it would never end!

Blossoms on the Ledge

I planted daisies in a pot,
A garden, small, but it means a lot.
They bloom with laughter, colors bright,
Tickling the wind, oh what a sight!

Along comes a bee, buzzing with glee,
He dances 'round like he's having tea.
I ask him to share some honey sweet,
He says, "Only if you offer me your seat!"

The petals sway as the breezes play,
A floral party in my day.
We laugh as the neighbors pass by,
"Are they on flowers or just getting high?"

What a grand show up here by my door,
With blossoms that sing and bugs that soar.
In this little garden, I find pure cheer,
Who knew joy could grow up so near?

Dreams in the Open Air

I sit and ponder, what a life,
Up here, away from the hustle and strife.
Clouds drift by, like marshmallows soft,
I reach out a hand, and then I scoff!

Below, the world spins—what's the next phase?
A cat in a hat chasing sunbeams and rays.
I imagine it all, a wild parade,
With fish on rollerblades, how absurdly conveyed!

The stars come out, not shy at all,
They wink at me from their cosmic ball.
"Join us," they seem to twinkle and say,
"In dreams, we dance the night away!"

So here I float, my thoughts run free,
In this open air, just my dreams and me.
With laughter echoing through the night's chilly breath,
I'll save my worries for a day of death!

Petals and Ponderings

Upon my ledge, petals drift down,
They twirl and dance like they own this town.
With each little swirl, a chuckle escapes,
As I wonder if flowers wear capes!

A butterfly flutters with such bold flair,
He flops down and says, "Do you have time to spare?"
"Let's plan an adventure, just you and me,
We'll float to the moon; it's as easy as tea!"

The sun nods along, a bright golden grin,
While I toss more crumbs to the next bumblebee kin.
Nature's confetti, it brightens my day,
In this lofty kingdom, I laugh and I play.

So if you're ever feeling quite low,
Join me above where the flowers glow.
With petals and thoughts that tickle the mind,
In my sky retreat, joy's what you'll find!

Enchanted? Above the Urge to Roam

In a garden that's bright with a shimmering sheen,
A squirrel in a hat starts planning a scene.
With acorns for gems, he invites all his peers,
To dance on the leaves while we sip on our beers.

Under skies full of laughs, where the daisies shout,
The bumblebee band plays a jolly route.
They polka with petals, they twirl and they spin,
While a ladybug winks, 'Oh, where have you been?'

A chorus of giggles escapes from the tree,
While the moon winks at nighttime, so silly and free.
With tickles and chuckles, we bask in delight,
No urge to roam when this wonder feels right.

So come join this frolic where laughter does bloom,
Leave your shoes at the door—this place is our room.
With nature's own jesters, we frolic until,
The stars start to yawn, and we glow with the thrill.

Solace in a Floral Oasis

Petunias are whispering secrets so sweet,
While the tulips engage in a dance with their feet.
A bee in a tux executes his grand twirl,
And the sunflowers giggle, 'Oh, isn't he a pearl!'

The breeze flirts with petals, it teases the vine,
As daisies declare that the day is divine.
A snail with a monocle sips dainty tea,
Saying, 'Life is more splendid when shared, can't you see?'

While butterflies boast of their latest designs,
The orchids all blush with vibrant new lines.
They chuckle and chat in the light that they seize,
Finding solace in blooms swaying soft in the breeze.

So let's wander together in this floral delight,
Where laughter is fragrant and everything's bright.
With petals as pillows and sunshine as laughs,
We'll stay in this garden and forget our paths.

Vistas of Calm Amidst Chaos

On a path paved with pebbles and dreams made of cheer,
A raccoon in glasses is all set to steer.
He nods to the flowers, those spunk-filled delights,
While the grass giggles softly at critters in flights.

The wind is a bard that tells tales of the day,
As clouds make a fuss, then drift on their way.
A duck in a bowtie conducts the grand scene,
While the frogs sing their notes—what a comical theme!

Amidst all the madness, a hammock it sways,
Inviting us gently in its dreamy ways.
You'll find calm in the chaos, just look for the fun,
And life will feel lighter, like clouds on the run.

So let laughter be lanterns that light up your path,
Where the curious critters concoct you a laugh.
With each step revealing a chuckle or two,
Who knew 'neath the chaos, calm joy could ensue?

Harmony on the Uprisen Path

In the shadow of whispers, the trees start to sway,
As a cat in a cape declares, 'Let's play today!'
With squirrels on skateboard, they zoom to and fro,
As laughter cascades from the streams down below.

Through the thicket of giggles and chortles galore,
A hedgehog narrates tales of the days of yore.
With stories of mischief that tickle the ear,
In this wondrous adventure, we draw ever near.

Rising high on the hills, with the sun on our backs,
We dance with the daisies; no plan or attacks.
Each step on the path held a jest and a jest,
In nature's own symphony, we're truly blessed.

So let's laugh a little and frolic a lot,
For joy is the treasure we've cleverly caught.
With harmony ringing and smiles on display,
Our uprise unfolds in the most fun-filled way.

The Garden's Perch

In a patch of green, I sit and grin,
Watching bugs dance like they just won a spin.
The daisies wink, gossiping low,
While squirrels plot to steal my show.

My neighbor's cat claims my sunniest spot,
As I shout, "Hey! That's my favorite lot!"
He stretches wide, all paw and tail,
While I sip tea, trying not to pale.

The grass tickles, it's quite a delight,
I pretend I'm a statue, frozen in sight.
But here comes the dog with his playful bark,
I leap like a fish, time to depart!

Yet in this fun-filled, breezy fair,
I cherish the laughter spun in the air.
With trowels and tales, we dance around,
In my little Eden, joy can be found.

Viewpoints of Tranquility

From my little ledge, I can see it all,
The neighbors play tag, I hear their call.
The tea's getting cold, but who cares for that?
I'm busy spying on the neighbor's cat!

A bird swoops by with a grand old song,
It lands near my chair, doesn't take long.
"Hey feathered one, fancy joining my team?"
He just cocks his head, like it's all a dream.

The wind blows gently, stirring my hair,
While I plot my escape from worldly despair.
With biscuits and jokes, I climb to the sky,
High on my thoughts, I'm ready to fly!

But here comes my plant, it's giving me shade,
As I laugh and rejoice in this lovely charade.
In this peaceful spot, life's worries take flight,
As I watch the world dance in morning light.

Above the Urban Chorus

High on my perch, city sounds below,
Horn honks and laughter, it's quite the show.
I catch a glimpse of a dog in despair,
Chasing his tail like he's lost in the air.

From my cozy nook, I spot a fly,
He's the king here, oh my, oh my!
With his grand parade across my jam,
I raise my glass, and call him 'Sam!'

Traffic is chaos, a zany ballet,
I laugh as I watch them display their ballet.
A pigeon lands close, with an attitude bold,
Sassy and brave, he's worth his weight in gold.

As rooftops and chimneys frame the craze,
I cradle my drink in this humorous haze.
With each honk and caw, I chuckle and cheer,
In this bustling theater, I hold my dear.

The Sun's Embrace

Basking in sunlight, I'm a lazy slug,
With a thumbs-up to rays and a cozy hug.
The flowers giggle, waving at me,
While I ponder how tall that tree could be.

A butterfly flutters, it tickles my nose,
Is it friend or foe? Only she knows!
With colors so bright, she steals the scene,
Making me feel like a summer queen.

As daisies play games in the breeze,
I watch their antics, I'm filled with glee.
A ladybug slips, makes quite the fuss,
Rolling like a ball without any bus!

So here I lounge in this sunny domain,
Laughing with petals, dancing with rain.
In this light-hearted garden, I find my bliss,
A moment of funny, I surely don't miss.

Embrace of Sunlit Terraces

On a ledge where the daisies dance,
The sun lands here, pulling off a prance,
Sipping lemonade, a cat on my lap,
Life's a riot, with a sunbeam nap.

Laughter bounces off the walls so bright,
While squirrels plot their stunts in delight,
They think they're kings of this sunny throne,
But I've got the snacks, they can't condone.

Up here, the clouds wear silly hats,
Trading gossip with my lazy pets,
The wind's a joker, tickling my ears,
While I'm mellowing out with my good cheers.

With each giggle, my worries grow small,
Sun-kissed shadows dance — oh, to have it all!
This terrace life is a wondrous caper,
Each hour here is a playful paper.

Nectar of Skyward Dreams

I sip from a cup of silly schemes,
Gazing up high, lost in sunbeams,
The sky paints stories, oh so absurd,
With clouds that giggle and rarely deter.

A bumblebee buzzes in comical haste,
While I munch on snacks, just a tad misplaced,
He's got more swagger than a fancy suit,
And here I am, in my old, floppy boot.

The sun's a clown, with its golden rays,
Tickling flowers in playful displays,
Each bloom is a buddy in this wild game,
Daring to dance and refuse all the fame.

With dreams that soar higher than my old chair,
I find joy in whispers of a balmy air,
In this realm of whimsy, my heart starts to beam,
Chasing the nectar of whimsical dreams.

Serenity Above the Garden

From a perch high above, the world feels right,
Beneath the green, there's a joyful sight,
Butterflies giggle as they frolic about,
While I place bets on who's had too much spout.

A rogue pigeon lands, acting quite bold,
As if sharing secrets, ancient and old,
He struts like a royal, unbothered by fate,
While I can't help giggling at myriad bait.

The herbs are chattering, 'It's quite a tease!'
As I sit and laugh at the buzzing bees,
A flower sneezes, and oh, what a mess,
It's easy to find joy in nature's jest.

Serenity reigns with a comedic twist,
Life's absurdity, something not to resist,
Above this bright garden, I'll stay all day,
Embracing the whimsy that comes my way.

Blossoms at the Edge of Day

As dusk falls, the blooms share a grin,
Whispers of petals as the day wears thin,
Crickets join in with a chorus of cheer,
While I spill my tea, laugh without fear.

Each flower's a joker, donning their hats,
Bending and swaying, while shooing away bats,
The evening light dances in hues of delight,
As I wiggle my toes, feeling just right.

Laughter bubbles up like a sweet summer brew,
In this garden of quirks, where whims never rue,
Fireflies flicker, their jokes lighting the way,
As blossoms keep chuckling, come what may.

At the edge of the day, where humor blends bold,
Nature's laughter, a story retold,
With petals and sunsets, my heart finds its play,
In this park of wonders, I gladly stay.

Blushing Blooms Above

In summer's sun, the flowers dance,
They wave hello, in funny pants.
A bee in shades, looks quite absurd,
While chatting loud, they form a herd.

With petals bright, and stems all spry,
They giggle soft, as clouds float by.
A gardener slips, with pots in hand,
The blooms all laugh, as if they planned.

In morning light, they strike a pose,
And wink at gnomes with silly clothes.
They have their tea on leaves so green,
While butterflies join in the scene.

A chorus sings of fun and cheer,
While squirrels dance, then disappear.
They puff out petals, just for kicks,
These blooms are quite the funny tricks.

Colors of Calm

In quiet hues, the flowers blush,
They giggle softly, in a hush.
A snail drags by, in quite the race,
While daisies chuckle, keeping pace.

The sun peeks in, with a bright grin,
While violets tease, and twirl their kin.
A cactus sighs, with prickly pride,
And waves to ferns, who dance beside.

With soft blue skies, the petals sway,
They trade sweet jokes throughout the day.
Each bloom a story, all its own,
In colors calm, they've brightly grown.

A breeze brings laughter, scents so sweet,
As flowers play, they skip retreat.
With every shade, a chuckle blooms,
In nature's laugh, all worry grooms.

Refuge in the Open

The daisies shout, they're open wide,
To pull in sun, and hide inside.
A petal falls, like feathered grace,
As blooms erupt, in wild embrace.

A butterfly slips, in splat of paint,
While garden tools play hide-and-seek.
The weeds just grin, they've come to play,
In this fun refuge, they'll surely stay.

The robin sings, a silly tune,
While tulips tap, beneath the moon.
With nature's laughter, all around,
It's the silliest spot, yet peaceful ground.

A patch of joy, amidst the green,
With laughter born, in every scene.
They scoff at hours, let laughter reign,
In airy refuge, where joy won't wane.

The Choreography of Flora

In the garden stage, blooms take their stance,
With petals twirling, they start to dance.
The sun takes lead, with a cheery glow,
While daffodils step, to the rhythm slow.

A gusty breeze, gives flowers flair,
The moves get wild, with fresh summer air.
Roses spin, with a curtsy grand,
While tulips support, with flowers hand-in-hand.

The daisies laugh, in a hop and skip,
Bringing charm, with a perp walk flip.
It's quite the show, no need for lights,
As blooms take turns, in delightful sights.

With nature's way, the stage is set,
In choreography, no bloom can fret.
It's a funny jam, in colorful show,
For flora's rhythm, forever will flow.

Whims of the Fluttering Leaves

Leaves dance in the breeze, oh so spry,
Giggling whispers beneath the sky.
They twirl and spin without a care,
Like children's laughter filled with air.

A squirrel joins in, with a wiggle and dash,
Plays tag with a bird in a light-hearted flash.
Nature's circus, a merry delight,
Where even the clouds chuckle, taking flight.

Sunbeams wink, playing peek-a-boo,
While daisies gossip in a fragrant hue.
The giggling grass ticks away the gloom,
Inviting all to join the bloom!

A butterfly's wiggle, a caterpillar's frown,
What a funny sight, in this leafy town.
With every rustle, the trees seem to giggle,
In a world where nature loves to wiggle!

Interlude with the Celestial Canopy

Stars play hide and seek, giggling so bright,
Moonbeams dance in the soft, velvet night.
A comet whizzes past with a cheeky grin,
Shooting stars wink, let the fun begin!

Clouds drift by, wearing fluffy white hats,
While owls hoot jokes like clever old bats.
The universe chuckles in whimsical ways,
As laughter echoes through starry displays.

A meteor shower's like confetti in flight,
Turning midnight solemn into pure delight.
Each twinkling gem whispers secrets galore,
In this cosmic playground, who could ask for more?

Galaxies swirl in a cheeky ballet,
Spinning joyfully, come join the fray.
With every blink of the distant sun's gaze,
The cosmos composes a humorous phrase!

Grace of the Flowering Outpost

In a corner of blooms where daisies take aim,
A bee with a buzz is seeking some fame.
With pollen-packed pants, he dances and grins,
Inviting the petals to join in his spins.

Tulips gossip with roses so fine,
Trading sweet secrets and flourishing wine.
The sunflowers stretch to reach for the sky,
As petals pose like models, oh my!

A ladybug skitters, her dots in a row,
Strutting her stuff, like she's part of the show.
With petals in tune, a flower power jam,
In this rosy stage, all nature's a fan.

Time pauses briefly in this fragrant retreat,
Where laughter and like-minded bloomers meet.
In this garden of giggles, delight's the decree,
Where flowers and friends can just be free!

Gardens Suspended in Time

In a whimsical patch where clocks take a break,
Garden gnomes chuckle by the old maple flake.
They sip on some dew, exchanging wisecracks,
Tickling the flowers as time gently backs.

Hummingbirds hover, with feathers ablaze,
Dancing in circles, in sundrenched displays.
With every sweet sip, there's a wink and a nod,
Nature's banter goes on, ever so odd.

Carrots and radishes, pranking their pals,
Hide-and-seek champions, oh what silly scalps!
While turnips twist through their muddy abode,
Playing the game of the infinite road.

With laughter that echoes through air fresh and fine,
This garden of joy, where the silliness shines.
In a world where minutes just love to unwind,
The secrets of happiness are sweetly entwined!

Skylines and Sweetness

Up high, I sip my fizzy drink,
Watching pigeons plot and think.
They coo with secrets, oh so sweet,
As crumbs invite their little feet.

A squirrel shows off its latest find,
With acorn treasures, truly unconfined.
I chuckle at its clumsy dance,
Nature's jesters in a nutty romance.

Clouds drift by like fluffy sheep,
While I bask in shade and take a leap.
The sun then winks, a mischievous glow,
I wave back, putting on a show.

My laughter echoes, lost in the breeze,
In these moments, life's sweet unease.
With every sip and every bite,
I find joy in this sunny delight.

Twilight's Kiss on the Patio

As daylight fades with a cheeky grin,
I dance alone, let the fun begin.
The stars emerge, wearing twinkly hats,
While crickets serenade, fancy a chat.

A moth flutters by with brazen style,
Dancing close, oh what a wild dial.
I joke, 'Are you looking for a light?'
It spins and swoops, what a silly sight!

The fireflies join, like tiny lamps,
My friends in summer's crazy camps.
We giggle as the night rolls on,
In twilight's glow, our worries are gone.

With snacks piled high in a jumbled heap,
We share our stories, our secrets to keep.
Laughter fills the air, oh what a blast,
In this patio realm, joy unsurpassed.

Celestial Reflections

Up on my perch, I survey the scene,
The stars are gossiping, looking keen.
They tease the moon, with a wink and a smile,
As I sit back, relaxed for a while.

A comet zooms past, with a trailing tail,
I wave and shout, 'You're a glorious whale!'
The cosmos giggles, a fantastic jest,
In this universe, I feel truly blessed.

Constellations whisper of tales untold,
Of heroes and legends, brave and bold.
I chuckle at Orion, his belt so neat,
Does he dual as a tailor? What a feat!

With stardust dreams, I drift away,
In this cosmic comedy, I long to stay.
Life's a reeling ride, a magical flight,
In these celestial wonders, pure delight.

Where Dreams Take Flight

High above the world, we rise and glide,
With pie in hand, what a joyous ride!
Birds join the feast, squawking in glee,
While I munch on my dream, carefree as can be.

A cloud drifts near, wearing a grin,
Inviting me over, where to begin?
I bounce from one thought to the next,
In this realm of whimsy, life feels perplexed.

I see a balloon, red and round,
Chasing after dreams that flip and bound.
My thoughts take flight, soaring up high,
While laughter rings out, as I touch the sky.

With a sprinkle of humor, and joy to ignite,
In this adventure, everything feels right.
So here's to the moments, both silly and bright,
In this magical space where dreams take flight.

A Seat Among the Clouds

I sat upon a plastic chair,
And thought, why have a millionaire?
The view was fine, the breeze a laugh,
I sipped my drink, a plastic half.

A bird flew by with sass and glee,
It chirped a tune just for me.
I waved hello, it did a twirl,
And knocked my snack - oh, what a swirl!

The sun shone down, a spotlight grand,
While ants gathered in a marching band.
They danced and pranced, oh what a sight,
Those tiny folks felt quite alright!

So cheers to chairs where clouds convene,
Life's better up here, or so it seems.
With snacks and smiles, the world feels bright,
In this high place, all feels just right!

Enchanted Vistas

Up high with snacks, my favorite treat,
I watched the world dance with my feet.
Cats plotted schemes from window sills,
While dogs just snoozed, ignoring thrills.

A playful breeze teased through my hair,
Where flowers whispered secrets, fair.
The view was vast, the sights were neat,
I spied a squirrel, what a cheat!

He snagged my chips without a care,
With little paws, he took the share.
I laughed as he danced back to his tree,
Guess he thought that all was free!

So here I am, in great delight,
With nature's joy, my heart takes flight.
Among the clouds and buzzing air,
I find my peace—no woes to bear!

Sunlit Corners

In sunlit nooks where shadows play,
I sip my coffee, greet the day.
With flowers blooming, colors bright,
Our garden crew takes off in flight.

The beetles march in perfect rows,
While butterflies flaunt all their clothes.
I chuckled once, and all was still,
As grasshoppers hopped with great goodwill.

A napkin flew, an unexpected guest,
So I missed a bit of my brunch fest.
"Not now!" I cried, as fowl took aim,
They dove and swooped, oh what a game!

Yet here I stay, in quirky cheer,
With all these antics, life feels dear.
From sunny seats, I glean the best,
In these bright corners, I am blessed!

Harmony Above the Ground

With a ukulele strumming near,
I filled the air with joyful cheer.
The neighbors chuckled from below,
As I sang loud, letting it flow.

A cat joined in with a modern spout,
He mewed in rhythm, a feline shout.
The sun winked down, a silly mime,
While squirrels danced to every rhyme.

Now who would think that up so high,
Harmony blooms with wings to fly?
Together we laugh, a wild ballet,
As clouds float by, in a breezy sway.

So here I strum, and life feels grand,
With furry friends, I make my stand.
Above the world, we lose the frown,
In this mad place, we wear the crown!

Fragrant Fables of Afternoon Light

In a garden where gnomes giggle,
Daisies dance with a sprightly wiggle.
Butterflies sip on sweet tea,
While ants plot a grand jubilee.

Lemonade spills on the green grass,
Squirrels race, oh how they pass!
Petunias wear hats made of dew,
Inviting each bee for a brew.

Sunshine tickles the hiding slugs,
While ladybugs give fierce hugs.
A cat naps under a wide-brimmed hat,
Dreaming of mice that are fluffy and fat.

As laughter floats through the air,
The flowers join in with flair.
Chasing shadows till the night,
In this funny garden delight.

Symphony of Colors and Climbing Vines

Vines twist like dancers, bold and spry,
Roses laugh, saying 'Oh me, oh my!'
Sunflowers bob to the bee's tune,
While petals giggle beneath the moon.

Loud frogs croak in a nighttime band,
While fireflies weave with a glowing hand.
Lettuce whispers secrets to the breeze,
As carrots giggle, 'We're such a tease!'

Chimes of color, all in a mess,
A bluebird lands to admire the dress.
With every chirp, a joke is spun,
In this garden where we share the fun.

Cucumbers wear shades, oh so cool,
While the tulips act like they rule the school.
Nature's laughter echoes so clear,
In this patch of whimsy, full of cheer!

Tranquil Heights where Wishes Bloom

Up on the hill, under a bright sky,
Wishes take flight, oh they seem to fly!
A bumblebee snickers at dandelion fluff,
Saying, 'Life's just a jest, isn't that tough?'

Clouds pass jokes as they change their shapes,
While critters gather to plan escapes.
A frog croaks riddles that make folk chuckle,
And rabbits hop, in disbelief they buckle.

Cacti tell tales with prickly flair,
And vines pull stunts without any care.
The brightest flowers share inside jokes,
As butterflies snicker at comedic pokes.

Amidst the stars, laughter ignites,
In this paradise of joyous sights.
Every wish whispered, floats to the moon,
In this tranquil height, we find our tune.

Garden Sentiments in the Breeze

In a patch where giggles grow wild,
Tulips gossip, each flower a child.
Petals whisper tales of the day,
In the breeze, they flitter and sway.

The scarecrow chuckles at a dancing beet,
As birds cartwheel on nimble feet.
A mud pie contest gets fierce and loud,
While earthworms cheer, forming a crowd.

Sunlight drips like honey so sweet,
While ladybugs win dance-offs on street.
In every corner, laughter surges,
As nature's joy constantly emerges.

Amidst the blooms, all wishes blend,
With humor tucked at every bend.
In this garden, the heart takes flight,
With sentiments swirling, pure delight.

Fragrant Horizons

In a garden of shoes, quite the sight,
Petunias in flip-flops just feel right.
Lemonade clouds float up high,
While squirrels debate the comfiest pie.

Butterflies with shades dance on the ground,
In hues that are lost and never found.
Each whimsy petal, a tickle or tease,
This wild patch of bliss makes no guarantees.

Sunshine giggles amongst the blooms,
Worms hosting tea parties with light-hearted tunes.
Beehives chuckle at the buzzing craze,
While daisies do yoga, lost in a daze.

So here's to the joys of this silly spree,
Where laughter and blooms invite glee.
Join in the fun, let your spirit mend,
In fragrant horizons where giggles transcend.

Windows to Paradise

Peeking through frames of clashing hues,
Llamas in pajamas, dancing in twos.
Marshmallow clouds serve lemonade drinks,
As turtles tip-tap, the sky winks.

Pigeons wear hats, they strut down the lane,
Making a fuss over spilt candy cane.
A snail on a skateboard flips with delight,
While butterflies snack on chips every night.

Sunlight spills coffee with cream and a dash,
As giggling daisies make their big splash.
Windows agape, the laughter flows,
In this land where whimsy endlessly glows.

So let's raise a glass to the quirky parade,
Of rabbits in suits and strawberries made.
Through these bright windows, let laughter ignite,
In a paradise playful, alive with delight.

Rooftop Reveries

On rooftops of laughter, we sit and we sway,
With monkeys in bow ties to brighten the day.
Kites made of dreams soar up to the sky,
While rainbows gossip, fluttering by.

We toast to the clouds with fizzy delight,
As rabbits on rooftops show off their flight.
Cats juggling yarn, oh what a sight!
In this topsy-turvy world, everything's right.

Sipping on sunshine, we dance with the breeze,
As owls in spectacles read books with great ease.
The stars throw confetti, they twinkle and gleam,
While hearts whisper secrets in a soft, silly dream.

So come join the revelry up high in the air,
Where merry mischief waits everywhere.
Rooftop reveries flourish, we delight in each whim,
In a symphony playful, on a cosmic whim.

Nature's Haven in the Heights

Balloons hitch a ride on the back of a breeze,
As squirrels serenade with a nutty tease.
Up here in the heights, where laughter takes flight,
Nature's haven giggles through day and night.

Pine trees don wigs, they boogie and sway,
While frogs in tuxedos croon on a tray.
Cherries throw parties, we're in for a treat,
As grasshoppers cheer with their tap-dancing feet.

A picnic of sunshine laid out with care,
As raccoons juggle pies, oh what a fair!
Glorious blooms, they stretch for the sun,
In this nature's haven, where whimsy is fun.

So let's make a toast to the joy we will find,
In the heights of this haven, light-hearted and kind.
Where each silly moment is a treasure to spark,
In nature's bright laughter, no room for the dark.

Harmony in the Airy Heights

In breezy spots where birds do flirt,
I sip my tea, with crumbs of dessert.
The squirrels plot with mischievous glee,
While I ponder life, and not just my tea.

A crow steals snacks, oh what a brat!
And leaves me pondering, should I be fat?
In this view high above the city's din,
I escape to joy—where does one begin?

The flowers dance, each petal a jig,
As I cackle loud; it feels quite big.
Bees buzz my tunes, a unique band,
In airy heights, the world feels bland.

So I laugh at clouds, they flinch at my cheer,
And in this funny realm, I hold dear.
Life's not too serious, up here I find,
In these breezy heights, it's joy unconfined.

Echoes of Nature's Sanctuary

Cheeky rabbits hop, they steal my hat,
While I chuckle softly, oh imagine that!
Nature giggles back, a ticklish breeze,
With snickers from trees, it aims to please.

The frogs in the pond throw quite the dance,
Hopping about as if in a trance.
I join their party, a jig on grass,
With echoes resounding, we twirl and pass.

Butterflies whisper jokes, fluttering bright,
As I try to catch them, oh what a sight!
The wind tells tales, all hazy and sweet,
In this sanctuary, my heart skips a beat.

So come laugh with me under the sun's glow,
In nature's embrace, we'll put on a show.
With echoes of joy and whimsy abound,
Here's to the laughter in nature we've found!

Views from a Celestial Ledge

Up on a ledge where the clouds feel near,
I shout to the stars, 'Hey, come grab a beer!'
With giggles from comets and winks from the moon,
I revel in this cosmic balloon.

A stray kite flutters, a bright paper friend,
Teasing the breeze, with no need to pretend.
I toss it some snacks, quite foolishly bold,
The laughter of legends—oh, stories retold!

The sun starts to blush, quite tickled at me,
As I dance with shadows and climb every tree.
Bubbles of laughter drift up through the night,
Creating a canvas of pure delight.

With views of the sky, a riot of glee,
I shout, 'To the stars! Come and join me!'
In this playful spirit, it's clear as can be,
Up here on this ledge, life sparkles with glee.

Lush Escapades Beyond the Rail

Beyond the rail where green vines twist,
I chase after plums; oh, what a tryst!
With critters conspiring, we frolic about,
In this lush escapade, we jump and shout.

The wind tells a tale of silliness grand,
As I chase the leaves, oh, isn't it planned?
I trip on a root, quite the clumsy affair,
Rolling in laughter, I just don't care!

Nature's my playground, absurdity's key,
As I swing from the branches, wild and carefree.
So grab your giggles and let kindness fling,
In the lush of the yard, where the silly hearts sing.

With berries and banter, let's savor the day,
In this vibrant jungle where we laugh and play.
So come join the frolic, let curses be pale,
In these lush escapades beyond the rail!

Whispers of a Crimson Horizon

A squirrel in a top hat, quite the sight,
Juggles acorns with all its might.
Birds chirp a tune, a raucous choir,
As butterflies dance, caught in a wire.

The sun spills laughter over the trees,
While ants march along with such ease.
A frog in a bowtie croaks a sweet song,
In this lively tale where everyone belongs.

A picnic unfolds, all food on the ground,
As a raccoon shows up, sneaky but sound.
Sandwiches stolen, napkins in tails,
An uproarious time where hilarity prevails.

At dusk, critters gather for a show,
A moonlit theater, with no tickets to throw.
Laughter echoes, the night takes its flight,
In this garden delight, where jokes ignite.

Secrets of a Verdant Vista

Caterpillars whisper, plotting a dance,
While flowers giggle, daring a chance.
A snail in a shell dons a fancy crown,
As dandelions puff, come on, don't frown!

Bees buzz a melody, sweet and bright,
While ladybugs waltz, a colorful sight.
A raccoon with sunglasses shades his eyes,
In a fashion show where all critters rise.

The trees share secrets, rustling with glee,
While shadows play games, a hide-and-seek spree.
A hedgehog in boots teaches the way,
To waddle and roll through the glamorous day.

As twilight unfolds, the jokes come alive,
With fireflies sparking, the insects all thrive.
A chorus of chuckles fills the cool air,
In this garden of wonders, laughter we share.

Petals in the Shade of Paradise

Under the daisies, a cat takes a nap,
Dreams of a fish, in a whimsical map.
Grasshoppers tap dance on stage of green,
While bees serve lemonade, sweet and serene.

A lizard in shades sunbathes with flair,
While shadows do yoga, stretching with care.
Hilarity blooms in the vibrant patch,
As daisies exchange gossip, what a batch!

The gnomes take a stroll, their hats all askew,
Chasing bright butterflies they think they once knew.
An old tortoise cracks jokes, slow but so wise,
While sunflowers giggle, tilting their eyes.

As dusk falls softly, the party ignites,
With frogs as the band under twinkling lights.
In this haven where joy takes its flight,
Laughter rings out, all through the night.

Reverie Amongst the Greenery

A hedgehog plays chess with a wise old tree,
While insects debate about who gets the tea.
The daisies gossip, spouting out news,
While butterflies flaunt their colorful hues.

Laughter spills out from under the ferns,
As the sun winks softly, today, it learns.
An owl in a bowler, playing the fool,
Makes everyone chuckle, a real golden rule.

A rabbit recites, poetry so bad,
Yet every creature laughs, not a bit sad.
In this patch of oddities, all heart and cheer,
Even the worms join in, how absurd, oh dear!

As night drapes a quilt over tales that we spun,
Crickets compose their symphony, one by one.
In the merriment found within leafy embrace,
Laughter and joy weave an unforgettable space.

Canvas of Sunbeams and Shadows

In a garden where daisies bloom bright,
A squirrel stole my sandwich, what a sight!
Bees buzz loudly, a raucous affair,
While I sip lemonade, without a care.

The sun paints stripes on my hat so fine,
A butterfly suits up, says, "This seat's mine!"
Laughter floats high with the sweet summer breeze,
As ants march by with a crumb, a tease.

My chair creaks loudly, a song it sings,
Telling tales of mischief and crazy flings.
With each goofy twist of my wobbly seat,
I find joy in every silly little beat.

So come, let's gather, bring snacks and cheer,
In this sunny spot, where the laughter's dear.
We may not be wise, but we're filled with fun,
In this joyful place, we all are young.

Reflections from an Elevated Haven

From my lofty perch, I give a shout,
To the cat that dangles, no doubt about.
She swings her paw like a mighty queen,
While birds plot schemes, like a feathery scene.

The clouds are fluffy, a cotton candy treat,
As I munch on popcorn, a savory feat.
A tiny gnome waves from beneath a fern,
With a wink and a nod, I take my turn.

The garden below is a circus of laughs,
With kids on scooters and muddy paths.
Every splash and stumble is caught in the air,
As I wave my flags, oblivious to care.

I chuckle at life, with its quirks and quirks,
Each moment a jester, with witty smirks.
So here's to the views that make laughter share,
From my elevated haven, nothing can compare!

Elixir of Twilight Petals

In the dusk, where flowers twinkle their eyes,
A rabbit brings tea, oh, what a surprise!
We toast to the stars, with cups in hand,
While the moon giggles soft across the land.

Fireflies dance like little glowing sprites,
As I tell ghost stories in funny bites.
The petals blush pink, with tales that they weave,
In this twilight haven, nothing to grieve.

My friends, the frogs, croak in harmony now,
With a choir of crickets, take a bow!
Each chirp is a punchline, a ribbit so bright,
As we bask in the giggles of the mysterious night.

So here we all sit, on this fragrant ground,
With laughter swinging, as dreams come around.
Each petal's a secret, each wink's a delight,
In our evening banter, everything feels right!

Escape Among the Wild Blossoms

In a place where wild blossoms tumble and grow,
A raccoon sneaks snacks, putting on a show!
I sip tea from flowers, so playful and bright,
Every sip bursts with giggles, pure delight.

The bushes hold secrets, of treasures and quests,
A scuffle, a shuffle, my hat's in the jest.
With laughter exploding like confetti in air,
Every breeze sings a tune, a charm to share.

A bumblebee buzzes, declaring it's prime,
Dancing round me, with rhythm, no time.
"Oh dear bee, please!" I chuckle and plead,
"Just don't land inside my herbal sweet tea!"

We chase down the sunset, with petals in hand,
In this wild escapade, we dance on the land.
So come join the fun, let worries all seep,
In this joyful disguise, where laughter runs deep!

The Lightness of Being

In a garden of socks and old shoes,
I dance like no one, with nothing to lose.
The daisies are giggling, they know my name,
I twirl with the squirrels, it's all a big game.

A cat on a chair gives a judgmental stare,
While butterflies flutter, without a care.
I juggle my dreams with a slice of pie,
Oh, lightness of being, just let it all fly!

The sun wears a hat, just to keep it all fun,
The daisies roll over, they're done with the sun.
I sip lemonade, on a whim I might swim,
In puddles of laughter, my chances are slim.

Tomorrow's a mystery, today's my delight,
With rabbit-shaped clouds, I'm soaring in flight.
The world is a joke, and I'm in on the play,
Embrace the absurd, it's a magical day!

A Touch of the Divine

The birds in their choir, they're hitting high notes,
I join in their jam, with my old winter coats.
The clouds are my friends, they're laughing up there,
As I trip on my feet, losing all of my hair.

I sip on my tea, but I spill on my shirt,
I think it's a sign, or just a dessert.
The moon winks at me, from the sky up above,
Could it be chance, or maybe it's love?

With each sketch of laughter, I craft my own fate,
The fruits of my folly, I happily sate.
In a universe wobbly, I'm dancing with grace,
A touch of the divine, in this silly old space.

So let's twirl in the chaos, and play like a kid,
With moments of madness, let all of it skid.
Life's but a jest, with sweet pie on the side,
Embrace the absurd, and let giggles collide!

Hummingbird Moments

A hummingbird zips, with a teeny-tiny hat,
It pauses to sip, then it's off—just like that!
I try to keep pace, but I'm more of a sloth,
In the race of my life, I'm losing my cloth.

The roses debate, on fashion and flair,
While the daisies throw parties, with free parking air.
I jump in the fun, all while wearing mismatched,
My secret's revealed, I'm a colorful batch.

With sprinkles of humor, I swirl on my chair,
The clouds are my audience, fluffing the air.
Each giggle's a flutter, each snort's a delight,
These hummingbird moments make everything bright.

Between giggles and hiccups, the time whirls away,
With sparkles of joy in the silliest way.
So dance with your heart, let your fun color blend,
In these hummingbird moments, we never shall end!

Beauty at New Heights

I climbed up a ladder, with socks that are bright,
To catch all the sunshine, it gave me a fright!
The flowers below, they all cheered with glee,
As I waved from the top, like a queen on her spree.

A bubble of laughter, it floated my way,
And asked for directions to join in the play.
With giggles as fuel, I soared like the breeze,
In my world of whimsy, I do just as I please.

The ants threw a party, I joined in their feast,
We laughed 'til it tickled, not one was a beast.
Zucchini balloons were the utmost delight,
We danced 'neath the sun, it was simply out of sight.

So if you should wander, up high, way up sassy,
Remember the journey always gets jazzy.
In beauty at heights, where all dreams unite,
Embrace every moment, and your heart will take flight!

Serenity of the Upper Floors

Up high where pigeons plot,
I sip my tea, it's piping hot.
The neighbor's cat gives me a stare,
Does he think I've turned to air?

Breeze tickles my toes, what a tease,
While I wave off wasps with great ease.
Clouds parade in fluffy gowns,
I wonder if they know of frowns.

Socks and sandwiches left to roam,
Comfy chaos feels like home.
With a book that laughs at me,
I nod and think, 'It's just a spree!'

A shoestring hangs from a starry shoe,
Who knows what mischief it might do?
Laughter echoes in the sky,
While butterflies giggle nearby.

Moments in the Breeze

A breeze that whispers silly rhymes,
Mixing laughter with sunny climes.
A hammock sways like a hammock should,
A gentle dance in the good old wood.

Sipping lemonade with a grin,
As ants march in a comical spin.
Giggling at the clouds that drift,
What a whimsically splendid gift.

Paper planes soar like wild dreams,
Chasing sunsets with joyful beams.
Maybe I'll join them, take to the air,
Who says a garden chair can't dare?

The sun's a jester above my head,
Spreading cheer where worries tread.
Here, jokes linger in floral cues,
Life's a circus with playful views.

The High Place of Thoughts

On a ledge where babbling thoughts,
Dance around like silly knots.
Daisies whisper their secrets old,
While daring bees also unfold.

Chasing ideas like children chase balls,
Laughing as laughter decorates walls.
Got a wild notion, perhaps a new shoe,
Or maybe a trampoline—who knew?

Clouds throw parties, each shape a delight,
Inviting me to join in their flight.
Scribbling jokes in the warm sun's smile,
Silliness waits to be shared for a while.

With quirks and giggles, plans must cease,
In this high place of light and peace.
Brainstorming giggles is such a thrill,
Let's toast to whimsy, oh what a skill!

Quietude in Greenery

Amidst the leaves, a squirrel debates,
If my chips are worth the waits.
He glances up with wide, round eyes,
As if to say, 'Could this be fries?'

The feathery branches sway and bend,
While laughter dances, a flawless friend.
Got my snacks and my dreams on hold,
As nature's stories gently unfold.

Flies buzz, they dance, they take a bow,
I chuckle, thinking, who taught them how?
Swapping fables with a curious frog,
Both of us living in comic fog.

Quietude wrapped in a cheeky spree,
Nature's laughter surrounds me with glee.
Here's to the silliness, wild and free,
In the greenery, joy is the key!

www.ingramcontent.com/pod-product-compliance
Lightning Source LLC
Chambersburg PA
CBHW050317100526
44585CB00016BA/1519